Dear Addictive Relationships

By: Aaron Fields

Copyright © 2020 Aaron Fields. All rights reserved.

Published by The Write Perspective, LLC

Dallas, Texas,

All rights reserved. No part of this book shall be reproduced or transmitted in any form or by any means, electronic, mechanical, magnetic, photographic, including photocopying, recording or by any information storage and retrieval system, without the prior written permission of the publisher. No copyright liability is assumed regarding the use of the information in this book. Even though every precaution has taken to prepare for this book, the publisher/author assumes no responsibility for errors or omissions. Neither is any liability assumed for any damage that results from the use of the information in this book.

ISBN: 978-1-953962-51-5

CONTENTS

Chapter 1 Addictive Relationships..1

Chapter 2 Emotional Hunger………………………………………………………..4

Chapter 3 How Bad Can It Get?………………………………………………….6

Chapter 4 No Self-Control……………………………………………………….8

Chapter 5 The Makeup Breakup Cycle………………………………………….12

Chapter 6 The Sex Trap…………………………………………………………18

Chapter 7 Being With The Wrong Person……………………………………… 20

Chapter 8 Is There Life Outside The Relationship?……………………………..22

Chapter 9 How To Overcome The Obsession…………………………………...25

Chapter 10 Make Yourself A Priority…………………………………………...27

Chapter 11 Are You Addicted To Someone?…………………………………….29

Chapter 12 My Advice To You…………………………………………………..32

Chapter 13 Final Thought………………………………………………………...35

Notes……………………………………………………………………………...

Something To Think About Before You Read

"In life, sometimes what we seek after is what ends up destroying us."

----------Aaron Fields

Word from the Author

When an individual is in an addictive relationship, he or she may have feelings of emptiness, hopelessness, and depression. A healthy relationship is not supposed to involve having obsessive thoughts about the other person. Relationships can become addictive because of the desire to stay connected with someone who you're not suitable for. Even though the person knows that the relationship is bad for them, they elect to stay, which can be dangerous.

A person who's in an addictive relationship will usually fantasize about their significant other too much. In most cases, the individual will give large amounts of their time, energy, and love. The absence of healthy boundaries in a relationship is clear when a person is ready to do anything or sacrifice everything to stay with their partner. If you're not careful, the relationship can become a hinderance and a detriment to your overall health and well-being.

Remaining in unhealthy relationships can be both physically and mentally harmful. Not only the toxic stress from an unhealthy relationship can drain your energy, but it can also increase the chances of a physical illness. Another major issue to be mindful of with these terrible relationships is that they can lead you on a dark path to drugs, alcohol, and even suicide.

Although there is a lot of pain in these types of relationships, most people stay, despite the negative consequences. Their brain is telling them to leave the relationship, but their feelings are making them feel helpless to take any action.

If you've never been subjected to this kind of relationship before, do everything in your power to avoid it. Once you get pulled into that addictive web, it becomes more difficult to come out of it.

Before you continue reading on, I want to take this time to encourage you to create a better life for yourself. Be willing to change and face the truth by overcoming any pain or past trauma that's inside of you. Remember, no matter what life throws at you, don't develop an addiction to shield yourself from the pain. That will only make matters worse. To maintain a healthy lifestyle, learn to function independently before starting a new relationship.

ADDICTIVE RELATIONSHIPS

Dear You,

Are you always checking your phone? Do you constantly think about someone? Are you tossing and turning every night in bed when you're alone? Do you always worry about what the other person is doing or thinking? If you answer yes for all of them, you are not alone because most people know what it's like being consumed by the thought of someone else.

Now when you love someone, it's normal to become preoccupied with the other person sometimes. Healthy relationships are one of the most important components to have in life. Believe it or not, both individuals can ease the hardships in the relationship. How? By consistently being supportive, respectful, loyal, and loving to one another. Some struggle to find peace when they become too fixated on the other person in the relationship.

Just like any other addiction, an addictive relationship will make you unstable. You'll also stop taking care of yourself in favor of the person you're addicted to. Are you really pursuing a healthy relationship that enriches your life? Or are you indulging in a relationship with someone that you can't live without? Most people in addictive relationships will use the other person to numb their pain. Why? Well, because they are covering a deeper level of agony that they refuse to deal with. This explains why most people seek relationships only to be rescued. They believe their relationship is filling a void inside of them.

The obsession you have with someone can become so intense that other important aspects of your life will suffer. Placing undue pressure and expectations on the other person may occur when you believe you can't survive without them. Feelings such as jealousy, anxiety, and insecurity can easily arise and develop in ways that can push the other person away.

Most people are not in healthy relationships because they are not comfortable learning how to be alone. Once you're able to explore why you feel dependent on the other person to make you whole, you will make the proper adjustments for a better life. You must be open to understanding what your underlying issue is really about. That way you can learn, grow, and understand how to accept real authentic love, rather than seeking certain relationships that are not right for you.

Let me ask you a question. Are you actually pursuing a healthy relationship, or are you indulging in a "love addiction" that you can't live without? To uncover the answer, you must do a self-examination. Reflect on your beliefs, behaviors, and motives. Please understand that who you are and what you do will attract certain people. Also, while you're at it, revisit your past. Most relationship addictions stem from early childhood or previous relationship experiences that went unhealed. The next step to finding out if you're seeking a healthy relationship or an addiction is to figure out if you can live without the other person.

A major thing to be mindful of in these addictive relationships is to never act in certain ways that will compromise your values and principles. Never allow a relationship to destroy you and always remember that you can never die from being single. Finally, never allow addictive relationships to steer you on a path to committing suicide or abusing drugs and alcohol. If certain things in your life spiral out of control, seek help.

2

EMOTIONAL HUNGER

Even though it's important to have a strong and healthy connection with the other person, having too much focus on them can be a serious problem. While you may think it's love, it could be feelings of emotional hunger. Most people attempt to satisfy their emotional hunger by relying on the other person. In most cases, this stems from emotional deprivation in the person's childhood. Part of the reason certain children cling to their parents is that they're not experiencing a strong connection. Therefore, the child becomes depleted, and it becomes more difficult for him or her to identify any love or truth in their life.

The pressure to make their partner feel complete stops them from feeling fulfilled in the relationship. Some people refuse to acknowledge that they have an excessive emotional dependency. They will often deny their insecurities by doing everything in their power to create a false narrative that they are "connected" to the other person. Perhaps this idea of belonging to someone eases their fear about the relationship and gives them a sense of immortality. Whatever the case may be, emotional hunger is a strong feeling and if you're not careful, this powerful emotion can be damaging.

Emotional hunger is a worldwide issue. If you're honest with yourself, you'll realize that the root of the problem to a large degree comes from you not knowing yourself. Not being connected to oneself can cause negative emotions and addictions. If you tested and assessed everyone, you'll notice that most of our problems result from a loss of a sense of self.

If you are driven by emotional hunger, you'll become unhealthily attached to others. Seeking validation from others may result from unresolved childhood issues. The reason I say childhood is that it's usually where the foundation of love and deep connected relationships start. Now, if you're among those who didn't experience love or develop a connection with someone, there is still hope. Although you may face difficult times, you can still break away from the behaviors that are keeping you captive. Do not allow yourself to be in a position that makes you unavailable to give or receive genuine love. Let go of your demons and explore what the world offers you.

3

HOW BAD CAN IT GET?

You might be in an addictive relationship if you continue to stay in one that involves abuse, control, or devaluation. As I mentioned earlier, most people already know that the relationship they're in is not good for them, yet they keep going back to the same person repeatedly. Does this apply to you? If so, it may be time for you to have a serious evaluation of the relationship you're in and seek some help. Never be in a relationship with someone that will cause you to doubt your self-worth.

As you seek meaningful relationships, always ask yourself the important questions. Does the relationship bring any value to your life? Can you grow mentally, physically, and spiritually? Are you in a relationship to avoid being alone? Can you function normally without being in a relationship? Most people in addictive relationships rarely ask themselves these questions. No matter what kind of relationship you are in, it should never be so controlling to where it takes away your ability to direct your own life.

What makes addictive relationships so dangerous? Well, not only do you lose sight of who you are and stop taking care of yourself, you also lose sight of your purpose in life. Therefore, you're no longer bringing out the best in yourself.

It's imperative to recognize the negative consequences that come with being in an addictive relationship. Sadly, most people don't realize it until it's too late.

So how bad can this addiction get? Well, let's just say if you ever question your morals, values, and integrity, then it may be time for the relationship to end. A healthy relationship will not only strengthen you, it will also help you move closer to your goals in life. Addictive relationships will move you off center because you're no longer aligned with your purpose.

Now let's further examine the consequences of being in an addictive relationship. As you continue to read on, you'll notice that being in a relationship filled with obsession and infatuation will cause you to act out in ways you won't be proud of. For example, let's say you're a kind and caring person, but you're constantly being castigated and mistreated in the relationship. Eventually, you could end up displaying the same toxic behavior towards other people. Always be mindful and aware of the energy that's around you because you never want to replicate the same behavior and turn into something that you despise.

4

NO SELF-CONTROL

Similar to any other addiction, a relationship addict has the inability to exercise self-control. Learning how to have self-control over your behavior and emotions are major steps for a person to take who's in an addictive relationship. If you're a relationship addict, you must regain power and control over your life and remember to be cognizant of how you react to certain situations. For example, let's say your significant other is cheating on you and abusing you. Instead of begging them to stop cheating on you, develop some self-respect by walking away from the relationship and moving on to something better. The essence of power comes from knowing your worth.

The first thing you need to understand about yourself and the relationship you are in is that you have to establish self-control. When you have self-control over your thoughts, emotions, and behaviors, others will value and respect you more. Also, having self-control makes you less likely to compromise your beliefs for other people. Therefore, to have self-control in a relationship, you will need to establish your values and your purpose. Don't come into a committed relationship until you have a solid understanding of who you are and what you are striving to become. Once you develop a strong identity, you'll be able to express what you want in a relationship more accurately. As a result, you will bring fulfillment not only to the relationship, but to yourself.

Overall, self-control is much needed for your health and well-being. Believe it or not, many people are unaware of their thoughts and actions. If you're not willing to scrutinize yourself, you could create a lot of problems in your relationships. Your life begins with self-awareness, so the more awareness you have, the better you'll be at controlling yourself.

Food for Thought: How to monitor your thoughts

Some of you have grown up in dysfunctional families and destructive environments. If this is true, it's likely that you did not receive the right tools, resources, and proper guidance you needed for success. Instead, you may have received the exact opposite. Unfortunately, your behaviors and thought patterns have led you to feeling anxious, angry, and depressed. Therefore, you have feelings of disappointment, sorrow, and emptiness.

The way you process the information life throws at you is going to be crucial to how you make it in this world. Think about how you view yourself, think about how you perceive and react to certain situations. If you are making poor decisions based on your dysfunctional thinking patterns, then you are not functioning at a high level. This kind of thinking negatively affects your job, finances, relationships, and your health.

Most of your ideas and decision makings are largely based on how you feel about yourself. If you are not careful about how you process information, your way of thinking will cause you emotional difficulties. Unfortunately, there are many children who come from broken homes. As a result, some of these children approach every aspect of their life with fear, anger, and self-defeat in their adulthood. Most people that are depressed feel helpless because they view their lives as something they have no control over. Perhaps this explains why having a strong culture is important. Many grew up in homes where their potential went unrecognized, preventing them from being their best selves. When you don't believe in yourself, life can become very problematic.

If you don't know where to begin, at least work towards feeling good about yourself. This will help you maintain power and control over your life. To be in the driver's seat of your life, develop a healthy mind.

5

THE MAKEUP BREAKUP CYCLE

Another sign of an addictive relationship is when multiple breakup and makeup cycles occur. Have you ever been in a relationship with someone that you could not stay away from for an extended period? Most people in an addictive relationship will keep coming back to their significant other, even when they know it's not healthy for them.

Being in the makeup breakup cycle can be mentally draining into the relationship. Have you ever started a reconciliation with someone after an argument, even when he or she was in the wrong? If you and your significant other keep breaking up with each other repeatedly, then maybe it's time to part ways and start working on yourself. Now some healthy relationships go through rough patches, but it's not repetitive and toxic. In my humble opinion, once you break up with them the first time, I wouldn't see the point in getting back together with that person because the issues you were experiencing initially are the same reasons the relationship didn't work out in the first place.

It's amazing how the pain of ending a relationship is so great that the individual will refuse to leave because they can't bear the idea of being alone. Although there is nothing wrong with being alone, many people become insecure when they're not with someone. You never want to walk on eggshells or feel desperate to keep the relationship alive when it was already dead to begin with. When you're not in a relationship, it's easy to feel lonely and abandoned. Most people who feel this way also develop this idea that they ruined the "one good thing" they had going well for them. Instead of beating yourself up for it, look at it as a new opportunity to become someone greater than what you previously were.

It's important for you to understand that being trapped in a cycle of love that's on and off is no way to live. Allow yourself to break the relationship off once and for all. By moving on, you can find someone else that will bring respect, loyalty, support, love, and happiness to your life.

One way to escape the makeup breakup cycle is to develop other parts of your life. Now what do I mean by that? What I mean is that you shouldn't allow the breakup-makeup pattern to consume all of your time and energy. Focus more on the other aspects of your life. That way, when you break up again, you'll have something to fall back on that will fulfill you as opposed to putting yourself back into the toxic relationship. Try investing more time with your family and close friends. Take on a new hobby, travel the world, revisit some of your old hobbies or anything else that pertains to fulfilling your purpose in life.

When you're in a breakup makeup cycle, you may feel as if your significant other is the only person in this world that will ever fulfill you. If you don't properly monitor your thoughts and emotions, you'll end up idolizing that person.

The reason you haven't found authentic love yet is because you're spending most of your time breaking up and making up instead of focusing on yourself. You can cultivate unique skills by learning how to be alone and take time to reflect on your life. When you're alone, read a book, write in a journal, cook, clean, or even meditate. Whatever the activity is, always show that you can have fun by yourself.

Have you ever been hesitant about ending a relationship because of fear of disappointing the other person or fear of not being liked anymore? Sometimes in life, letting go of something or someone detrimental to you can be the best thing to happen. There is nothing wrong with letting go of something that's unhealthy for you. Eventually, there will come a time when you will have to tell the other person the relationship is over. Whether the two of you decide to no longer stay in contact anymore or not see each other temporarily is totally up to you. Whatever you do, don't keep in close contact with the other person if you're just going to keep hashing out the same old problems. The more you continue to live in the past, the harder it becomes to live in the present.

Now listen, most of us have been through on and off relationships and that's okay, because life is about going through a series of learning experiences. However, if you're always in a makeup breakup relationship, that means you do not know what you want out of life. Think about it, on and off relationships mean that you and your significant other are starting major conflicts with each other.

The relationship is in such a terrible state that you'll break up for a long time, reconcile, and then repeat the cycle. I want to make you aware that toxic relationships are not healthy and won't last. As soon as you recognize that you're in this kind of relationship, do yourself a favor by removing yourself from that toxic situation. If you don't, it'll only get worse.

The things that upset you in the relationship are the same things that sustain the makeup-breakup cycle. One minute you see all the red flags and become determined to leave the relationship and the next minute, you suddenly talk yourself out of it. Why? What are you afraid of? In this activity, I need you to take the time to write about all the things that upset you about the relationship that you were or are currently in. When you write, make sure to mention your thoughts, emotions, and the efforts made or not made by both of you to resolve the issue.

_____

_____

_____

_____

_____

_____

_____

_____

_____

_____

_____

_____

_____

_____

_____

_____

_____

_____

_____

*After you finish writing, read it over a few more times and then reflect and internalize the information you just wrote. It's very important for you to recognize and understand that you will not escape your problems just by getting back together with that person. As you continue to meditate on this matter, always remind yourself of the recurring issues that never seem to improve in the relationship. Why do I say this? Well, because most people look the other way and ignore the red flags.

6

THE SEX TRAP

There is a tremendous difference between sex and love. Most individuals in addictive relationships usually confuse the two. Just because someone is having sex with you doesn't mean they value the relationship. Have you ever seen a relationship where every time abuse was involved, the couple would try to resolve the problem by having sex? If you have, that is what you call an unhealthy and addictive relationship.

I understand that it's challenging to stay focus and maintain self-control, knowing that sex can take place anywhere and anytime. When you're attracted to someone, your body will give off certain chemical reactions. This will make the opportunity to have sex with someone you're attracted to much harder to resist. The powerful chemical reactions lead to feelings of excitement, love, attraction, and closeness. If you're in an addictive relationship, you can't allow these feelings to put you in a sex trap. When this happens, you'll prioritize physical intimacy and ignore the other aspects of the relationship. If you're not paying attention, you'll end up saying something silly like, "Well, even though we have a lot of unresolved issues in our relationship, at least the sex is great".

To avoid falling for this trap, you must understand what you want versus what you need. Just because you have sexual urges doesn't mean you have to act on them. Although sex is a great spark in the relationship, there are many other components to a relationship that are just as important. Overall, there is no such thing as a healthy relationship without having values and a vision.

7

BEING WITH THE WRONG PERSON

What makes certain relationships so tough is that noticing the wrong things is not always obvious. It's impossible to pinpoint others' errors unless you clearly understand yourself and your values. Did you know some people are actually more afraid of being alone than they are of being with a dangerous person? If this applies to you, consider finding new values and addressing deep-seated issues you have.

What was your childhood like? Do you come from a broken family? Are you surrounding yourself with toxic people? When you're carrying unresolved issues, you'll lose sight of how you value yourself. Without having the capacity to love yourself, you cannot establish who you really are.

When you find yourself in a relationship with a dangerous person, you risk putting up with verbal, emotional, or physical abuse. Unfortunately, the relationship can get so toxic that when it ends, both people can become damaged. As soon as you realize you're with the wrong person, just leave the relationship and stop wasting time. Staying in a toxic relationship too long will not only lead to poor decision making, but you'll also lose a strong sense of your own identity.

What makes most relationships so dangerous is that it can turn into a clinging, possessive, and overbearing situation. This relationship will only add pain and distress to your life. Let's be honest, you have an addiction because you are more interested in the idea of being with someone and you don't want to be alone. Never force yourself into a relationship that is not meant to go well for you.

If you ever imagine the person's potential rather than focusing on who they are, then you're on the verge of self-sabotaging the relationship. It's not healthy to create a fantasy in your mind because eventually, you'll have to stop ignoring the realities of your circumstances. It's easy to keep going back to the same relationships that will hinder you. However, it's much harder to surround yourself with positive people that will bring out the best in you and hold you accountable. Develop some courage and learn when to let go of relationships that were never suitable for you. If you want to be with the right person, start off by getting to know your true self first.

8

IS THERE LIFE OUTSIDE THE RELATIONSHIP?

Most people in addictive relationships smother the other person by giving up too much of their time, energy, money, and love. Have you ever lost interest in your job, friends, family, or a hobby over a significant other? Relationship addicts often neglect other aspects of their life, as their entire focus is on the relationship, even if the other person isn't invested. Are you willing to lose everything for the sake of keeping a meaningless relationship? If you find yourself not being able to manage your life outside of your relationship, then it sounds like you don't need to be with anyone right now.

The more you neglect yourself, the more exhausting your life can become. Having a life outside of the relationship will allow you to have better control over your happiness. Not only is being happy on your own builds confidence, but it also creates character. Plus, you won't feel obligated to maintain an unhealthy relationship with someone.

If you're one of those individuals that believe there is no life for you outside of the relationship, try getting into different hobbies. Have you ever played a musical instrument? Do you read or paint? If you are completely stuck and can't think of anything, think about some things you used to do when you were a kid.

Still struggling with hobbies? Well, have you ever considered having a spiritual connection with God or a source of a higher power? Perhaps the only source of peace, love, and joy comes from having a beautiful spirit. Developing a spiritual connection with God can be the most important component to building a strong and purposeful life.

Find Your Purpose Activity

Before you initiate yourself into a serious relationship, find your true identity and think about what you want out of life.

What do you want to be? _____
_____
_____
_____

What do you want to do with your life? _____
_____
_____
_____

What are you gifted at? _____
_____
_____
_____

What tools do you need to be the best version of yourself? _____
_____
_____
_____
_____

9

HOW TO OVERCOME THE OBSESSION

It's difficult to overcome an addiction on your own. Just like drug addicts, relationship addicts will need help and support. Getting professional help from someone that knows what they're talking about can be the best thing you can do for yourself. If you're experiencing relationship issues, specialized counselors and mentors can provide valuable support.

Anything that becomes addictive to you, no matter how clean or untainted it is, it does you no good, especially in relationships. Look, I understand that ending a relationship is hard, but in order to reach levels of prosperity in your life, things will have to change. Stop beating yourself up and get over that desperate need.

If you've had previous relationship issues or grew up in a dysfunctional environment, overcoming this addiction may be much harder for you. Why is that? Well, because you've never seen what a healthy relationship looks like. However, that doesn't mean it's impossible to overcome. All you need to do is have the willingness to change for the better by understanding the importance of healing and repairing your life.

The first step you need to take in the healing process is to face the truth and acknowledge that you have an addiction. Before you can overcome any addiction, you must admit that you have a problem first. Also, never take your feelings, thoughts, and desires for granted. Sometimes, your thoughts and emotions can offer an accurate reflection of all the things that have transpired in your life.

Another way to overcome an obsessive relationship is to never depend on the love of another person. The most powerful love comes from you loving yourself. Allow no one to treat you with disrespect. There is nothing wrong with establishing healthy boundaries.

10

MAKE YOURSELF A PRIORITY

It's natural to want to speed up the healing process when you see improvements in your life after leaving the addictive relationship. You'll probably want to make up for the things you missed out on, like spending more time with friends and family, or maybe traveling around the world. Although those things are great, don't forget to prioritize your needs first.

When it comes to setting your priorities, think about how you spend your time. When you're prioritizing your life, use a sizable portion of your time thinking and learning alternative ways on how to elevate yourself. Take the time to reflect on the things you consider more important to you. While you're at it, list a few short-term and long-term goals you'll like to achieve.

With your family and friends, seek their support. Believe it or not, sharing your pain with friends and family can make your situation more manageable. Allow them to be there for you and let them protect you. Don't even think about hiding your situations from them just to make things look "better" than what they actually are. Have a support system and you'll be surprised how much it can stop you from getting in your own way and ruining your life.

The goal of making yourself a priority is to develop a better life with new habits that will keep you from relapsing. Although it's natural to feel disturbed and guilty about the past, it's also natural to move on to better things. Don't spend too much time living in the past because you'll end up neglecting the future.

It's inevitable that learning how to prioritize your life is going to take some time. Even with all your new goals that you plan on achieving, it is still essential you don't aim too high right off the bat and overwhelm yourself. In the meantime, continue to attend therapy, seek help, and always find different ways to self improve each day. Remember, great things take time to build.

11

ARE YOU ADDICTED TO SOMEONE?

How can you tell if you're addicted to someone? Initially, you may not detect it at first because, just like drugs, there is an intense feeling. Remember, the person you adore so much can also belittle you, abuse you, and make you feel worthless. First, you'll question yourself and wonder how you got involved in this situation. Then you might make a declaration that you'll never tolerate this type of abuse again, but as with any other addiction, it'll make you keep coming back.

Before you even realize how deep you are in this unhealthy relationship, you will find yourself frustrated, depressed, and confused. If you're at a point in the relationship when you're not willing to let that person go, even though they've treated you horribly, then you're in too deep. Don't be shocked if you have to put up with anything that's being thrown at you. Although you recognize this situation is detrimental to you, you can't help but reminisce about the good times you've had with that person.

It's difficult to protect yourself from this kind of addiction because it takes a lot of time and willingness to build self-awareness. It's imperative to see things for what they really are instead of normalizing ill-treatment. To keep yourself out of harm's way, do not develop an infatuation and a physical need to be around a specific person. If you are not the best version of yourself when you're around that person, find out why. Looking for love in a relationship doesn't happen instantly. It takes time and a mutual effort from both sides. So before you quickly jump into something, take a step back and think it over. Are you really interested in getting to know somebody, or are you just looking for an immediate fix?

A major rule to know about being with other people is to not be impulsive. Think things through in every situation, and just because you want something out of a relationship doesn't mean you have to accept more bad than good. It's not rational to mistreat someone, then shortly after, pretend to care about you. Always pay close attention to how you truly feel about certain people. You also want to keep in mind that you need great reasoning skills too in order to remain objective about the people you're dealing with. Always view people for what they actually are instead of what you wished them to be.

You and others already know that getting out of an addictive relationship is tough. Interestingly, you might not even notice your addiction until you finally sit down and reflect on your life. It's hard to imagine the fact that people can become addicted to another person, but once the addiction is identified, everything else will make sense. You'll start understanding why you keep selecting the same person; you'll start understanding why you continue to search for that immediate attraction. Eventually, you'll know why you keep allowing yourself to come back to the same toxic relationship.

12

MY ADVICE TO YOU

My suggestion to you is to pay attention to the physical, psychological, and emotional feelings you're experiencing. Speak to someone that can help you with your situation. Also, be willing to listen and comprehend the things people tell you, even if you don't want to hear it. Now, this won't be easy to achieve, especially if you're already addicted to the relationship you're in. However, as you continue to pull away from your addiction, you'll start seeing things for what they really are.

Never take an addiction for granted. In certain relationships, you can even become addicted to the fighting aspect of it because you crave for that adrenaline rush. Have you ever thought about using that same energy and excitement with someone who will treat you like a human being? Why do you feel the need to always engage in combat with the other person? Is it because it turns you on? Trust me, I understand, but just because it's a turn on, it doesn't mean it's healthy for you. Remember, there is always a better way to handle certain conflicts. Whether it's feelings of pain, anger, sadness, fear, or emptiness, always take the time to regulate and navigate through your emotions. You can accept this belief or not, but there's always a reason you act a certain way.

Finally, understand that the only person who can change in the relationship is you. Stop getting so fixated on how the other person needs to change. Understand that you have no control over the other person. Wanting someone to change is only giving you more of a reason to remain hooked and addicted to them. The most beneficial action is to practice self-compassion through positive reframing and self-belief.

I Promise Activity

One of the most fulfilling things you can do for yourself is sticking to your promises. Whatever promise you make to yourself, take it seriously, especially if it's meant to improve your mental health. In this activity, take the time to read each promise and internalize each principle. Use this information and apply it to your life the best way you can.

I promise to be objective and use reasoning skills in my decision makings

I promise to live one day at a time

I promise to remove myself from a toxic person

I promise to regulate my emotions

I promise to no longer engage in no-win arguments

I promise to never ignore my feelings

I promise to get in touch with a trusted person if I ever feel physically, emotionally, or spiritually unstable

I promise to love and value myself

I promise to never give up on myself, even if others do

What did you learn from this activity and how did it make you feel?

_____
_____
_____
_____
_____
_____
_____
_____
_____

13

FINAL THOUGHT

Your love addiction doesn't necessarily have to be related to a romantic or sexual partner. It is possible to have addictive relationships with friends, children, or even public figures whom you have never met before. Don't plan on getting with someone with the assumption that the other person is going to solve all of your problems. If you're not careful, you'll end up becoming bitter towards that person because they didn't meet your needs.

The beauty of overcoming these addictions is the process of self-discovery. Self-discovery should be an important goal for you to reach if you haven't done so already. The reason self-discovery would be essential to anyone is because most people are going through life trying to play a role that doesn't fit them. Because people don't know themselves, they try to become what they think others want them to be, rather than identifying with their own purpose.

The irony of this "love" addiction is that it really isn't about love at all. It's more of an unhealthy obsession full of arguments, fights, jealousy, mind games, guilt, manipulation and emotional tear downs. Yet you keep coming back to it. Why is that? It's simple; you're addicted.

There is nothing wrong with wanting to be with other people emotionally, physically, and spiritually. For most of us, life is a lot better when you share it with someone special. However, if you don't monitor your thoughts, the feeling of loving someone can become addictive. Becoming addicted to someone may sound cute and romantic at first, but if you're not careful, it'll turn into something toxic. Before you ever deal with someone on any level, consider what a healthy relationship looks like for your life.

I hope you understood the message of this book and the importance of it. As it pertains to any addictive relationship, don't live your life trying to make the other person happy because you'll never reach the highest potential of what you can be. It's imperative that you grasp the fact that life is about constantly growing and changing for the better. To do that, focus on what you want to be and understand the importance of knowing how to be by yourself. If you don't understand how essential it is for you to be alone, you'll never fully know how to be self-driven. When you're not self-driven, you risk getting manipulated your entire life. Understand your purpose, know what your goals are and take time to be by yourself because ultimately that's part of the human experience.

To become a champion in life, another thing you have to do is stop carrying around your emotional baggage. I understand bad things happen whether it was in your childhood, or previous relationships, but whatever baggage you have, you need to let it go so you can grow. If you keep holding onto the negative things that took place in your life, your unresolved issues will continue to occupy your mind and body. As a result, your emotional baggage will interfere with your ambitions, and in every relationship you go into, all just because you didn't know how to move on. Why are you thinking and running back to old things that are not benefiting you? Instead of letting your past hinder you, just live better and train yourself to be a forward thinker. You cannot be a benefit to anyone else if you're not a benefit to yourself.

Sincerely,

Aaron Fields

Notes